A Walk by My Side

JOURNEYS THROUGH NATURE AND SOUL

BHAVYA RAJENDRA

To the Almighty, this book is devoted, with profound reverence

Contents

Contents

Foreword

In the realm of poetry and prose, there exists a delicate dance between words and emotions. It is within this realm that Bhavya dwells, blending thoughts and feelings that captivate the soul.

As I embark on this journey through Bhavya's collection, I am reminded of the profound power of language to evoke emotion and provoke introspection. Each piece is a testament to her keen observation of the human experience, sprinkled with authenticity and grace which is truly remarkable.

But what distinguishes Bhavya's work is its accessibility. Her poetry transcends barriers, resonating with readers of all backgrounds and levels of literary experience. With simplicity and clarity, she articulates universal thoughts and emotions, inviting even the most casual readers to engage and connect with her words. Whether you are a seasoned bookworm or a first-time reader, Bhavya's writing effortlessly bridges the gap between hearts and minds.

In these pages, you will find solace, inspiration, and above all, a profound sense of connection to something greater than ourselves.

So, dear reader, come, have a walk by her side, and open your heart and mind to the beauty and wisdom contained within these pages.

For in them, you will find not only a celebration of the written word, but also a celebration of life itself.

With warmest regards,
Nirmal Sridharan

Acknowledgements

I am deeply grateful to my husband, **Rajendra Kumar**, whose incredible support and never-ending love have been my anchor throughout this journey. Your unwavering encouragement and belief in me have fueled my passion for writing, and I am endlessly thankful for your presence by my side, always motivating me to pursue my dreams.

To my darling daughter, **Aadhya**, your presence fills my days with joy and inspiration. Your boundless love and understanding have been a constant source of strength, motivating me to pursue my dreams wholeheartedly.

To my beloved parents, **Gayathri** and **Babu**, and my dear sister and brother-in-law, **Divya** and **Naveen**, your love, support, and unwavering belief in me have shaped me into the person I am today.

A heartfelt thank you to my father-in-law, **Namdev**, and my late mother-in-law, **Komala**. Your support and blessings have been immensely appreciated.

To my dear friends, **Laura**, **Roopa**, and **Mahantagouda**, your continuous guidance and motivation have been invaluable to me. Your belief in me has kept me going during the toughest of times, and I am incredibly grateful for your unwavering friendship.

ACKNOWLEDGEMENTS

A special thanks to my mentor, **Nirmal**, for guiding me every step of the way. Your wisdom, encouragement, and invaluable insights have been instrumental in shaping this book, and I am deeply grateful for your mentorship.

Heartfelt thanks to **Notion Press** for their support and assistance, making this journey a smooth and rewarding one. Your professionalism and dedication have made all the difference, and I am truly grateful for your contribution to this project.

And to you, **Dear Reader**, thank you for embarking on this journey with me. May the words within these pages resonate with you and bring you solace, understanding, and inspiration. This book is dedicated to each of you, for your unwavering support and belief in the power of poetry.

Prologue

Welcome to a journey through the heart's whispers and soul's musings—a collection where poetry and prose intertwine to paint the canvas of human emotions. Through these verses, I aim to offer solace and connection to those who feel alone in their experiences. Each poem is a reflection of the diverse emotions and struggles we all face, reminding us that we are not alone in our journeys.

Poetry has been my refuge, a means of expressing my innermost thoughts and feelings. However, my journey as a poet has not been without its challenges. At times, I found myself hesitant to share my work, fearing the judgment of those around me. Yet, despite the doubts and uncertainties, my love for writing poetry persisted, driving me to continue putting pen to paper.

In this book, you will find poems born from moments of joy, sorrow, love, and longing. They are a testament to the human experience, a reminder that our stories are intertwined, and our voices are worthy of being heard. So, as you journey through these pages, may you find solace, understanding, and a sense of unity in the shared threads of our collective experiences.

Note To The Readers

• xiii •

Readers are kindly asked to note that the poems are presented without any particular order.

Each poem is accompanied by an exposition from my perspective; I encourage you to peruse these insights as well.

1. Magic in the Night sky.

A dark night, comes a gentle breeze.

Staring at the sky, I lay freeze.

Thoughts like lightening,

Flashing everywhere.

I abandon them as they don't belong to the serenity.

Mother Earth embraced me, As I lay in her arms.

A shooting star insists I make a wish.

And how I wish it come true.

The leaves whisper to me, Oh!! I already have secrets within.

Laughs a little birdie and shows me how she flies.

And there is the moon watching everything, with her infectious smile.

Spreading love and joy as she grows smaller.

Cause she knows it is never the end...

Isn't it amazing how the night feels different from the day? I like it when the sun sets and everything starts to calm down. You can see birds going home and the sky turning dark. It's like the world is taking a break after a busy day.

At night, everything feels peaceful. Sometimes I just want to lie down and look at the sky. It's so quiet, and if you listen carefully, you can hear the stars twinkling.

The night carries with it a certain magic, a reminder that there's beauty to be found in the darkness. It whispers to us to let go of the worries of tomorrow and to find solace in the peace of the present moment. The night is special because it's not scary like some people think. Instead, it's calming and makes us feel safe.

So, let's embrace the night, with all its mysteries and wonders, knowing that within its depths lies a gentle calmness waiting to be discovered.

2. Bedtime Bunny on the Moon

I see a rabbit on the moon, snug in its bed.

Hushing away with worries and dreams unaddressed.

Every new moon I await, to stare into the sky.

Wanting to see the rabbit fly high high high!!

Whenever I gaze at the moon, a peculiar sight captures my attention—a rabbit, nestled within its luminous glow. This image, though whimsical, carries profound symbolism, representing the concealed worries and aspirations we harbor within.

The sight of the rabbit on the moon evokes a sense of comfort and ease, as if it has found refuge from the cares of the world. Observing these celestial rabbits, I'm reminded of the importance of creating a sanctuary amidst life's uncertainties, where we can momentarily set aside our burdens.

Anticipation builds with each cycle, as I eagerly await the arrival of the new moon—a symbol of fresh beginnings and the renewal of inner strength. Gazing at the moon offers a glimpse into the depths of one's soul, stirring a yearning for transformation and a desire to transcend life's challenges to achieve greater heights.

3. Seaside Stroll

The gushing water, the roaring sea
Waves hit the shore and touch our feet.
Washing away the castles built on the sand.
Watching the tides, walking with you hand in hand.

In every wave, a story is spun,
As the sea whispers for everyone.
When you stroll beside me, along the shore
There are stories discovered forever more.

Have you ever experienced the serene beauty of a beach at dawn? It's truly magical. As I sit here, I can almost feel the crisp morning air brushing against my skin.

• 6 •

I recall a memorable family trip when we had the privilege of staying in a private beach villa. We were told that the beach was exclusively for resort guests, ensuring a peaceful and uncrowded experience.

The n ext m orning, w e e agerly r ose e arly t o m ake t he most of our time on the beach. Watching the sunrise, feeling the cool breeze on our faces, and the soft touch of the cold sand beneath our feet—it was all incredibly blissful. It's a feeling that words alone can't capture, only experienced first-hand.

So, why wait any longer? Consider packing your bags and embarking on a getaway. Perhaps it's time to nudge your partner for a well-deserved vacation.

4. Oceans Embrace

• 7 •

I gaze upon the oceans; I smell the breeze.

How sweet and nostalgic, the waves cooling my feet.

Strolling along the shore, with sand between my toes

Then I awaken, realizing it was all just a dream that softly

goes.

At times, we all dream of a calm and easy life, like sitting quietly on a beach. We wish we could feel that same calmness in our daily lives, just like the comforting feeling of wet sand between our toes.

There are moments when we simply crave the freedom to stroll without burdens, confident that all will be well and challenges will be manageable. We indulge in daydreams of carefree confidence, feeling capable of conquering any obstacle in our path.

Yet, reality often reminds us that some dreams may remain just that—dreams. It's like picturing something delightful, only to confront the possibility of it never materializing. Despite this realization, we can still cherish life's simple pleasures and find solace in fleeting moments of peace.

5. Ice-Cream Dreams

An Ice-cream cart, going around,
Ringing the bells, to hear the sound.

Can you hear the Cling-Clang,
Of your little piggy bank.

Running then began,
Not to miss the ice cream cart.

Popsicles or scoops, which one to choose?
So many flavors, and I am so confused.

Here comes the candy ice cream that I want.
Savouring every bite as I hold it to flaunt.

When will you come again, longs the heart,
Feeling dejected I let go of the cart.

Waiting for the popsicles, to freeze my tongue.
And delight in another day filled with so much fun.

As a child, running towards an ice cream cart was always a thrilling experience. I would hear the bells ringing, announcing the arrival of the cart, and it was like music to my ears. The sound would instantly remind me of the coins in my piggy bank, ready to be spent on a sweet treat.

Once the cart came into view, my excitement would reach its peak, and I would dash towards it without a second thought. There were so many choices to pick from - popsicles or scoops, each with its tempting flavors.

Savouring every bite of the delicious treat, I would proudly hold it up for everyone to see, feeling a sense of joy and satisfaction. As the ice cream cart moved on, I would watch it disappear into the distance, longing for its return. Yet, despite the fleeting nature of the experience, I knew that there would always be another day filled with fun and delight, waiting just around the corner.

For those reading, I hope these words stir up memories of their own childhood experiences with ice cream carts - the excitement of hearing the bells, the thrill of choosing a flavor, and the joy of savoring every delicious bite. May we all cherish these sweet moments from our past, and look forward to creating new ones in the future.

6. Parkside Memories

A walk in the park, watching children play
Nostalgia stirs memories of when you were happy and gay.
Sandwiches and candy; slides, and many rides.
All day gone, not wanting the dance to glide.

Strolling in the park, and watching kids play, brings back memories of my happy childhood days. It's like going back in time, feeling the joy and laughter I used to have.

• 12 •

I remember the simple pleasures, like eating sandwiches and candy and enjoying the slides and rides at the park. Those carefree moments seemed to last forever, and I didn't want them to end.

Now, as I watch children playing, I can't help but feel nostalgic for those times. It's a bittersweet feeling, reminiscing while appreciating the present. Those childhood memories will always hold a special place in my heart, reminding me of the innocence and happiness I experienced during those carefree days.

7. Seascape Serenity

A vast spread of water,
Where there is shallow and there is deep.
It's mighty and majestic,
What else can you feel?

The turquoise water is so blisses to be,
The frothy waves touching your feet.
The cool breeze, the choppy waves,
The oceans and its friends I see.

The serene beauty, the brackish waters.
The sight that never ends.
The magnificent enchantress and its changing spirit,
Sometimes calm and sometimes perilous.

The ocean, like life itself, has its ups and downs. It's like a giant playground, where you can find both shallow spots to paddle in and deep areas to explore. Sometimes, it feels calming and inviting, like a warm hug from nature. You can imagine dipping your toes in the cool, turquoise waters and feeling the gentle waves tickle your feet.

But just as life can throw unexpected challenges our way, the ocean can turn wild and unpredictable. Picture standing on the shore, watching the waves crash against the rocks, and feeling the wind whip through your hair. In those moments, you realize the immense power and vastness of the ocean, and it reminds you that nature is both beautiful and formidable.

Despite its dangers, the ocean draws us in with its endless possibilities and captivating allure. It's a reminder that life is an adventure, full of both calm seas and stormy waters. And just like sailors navigating the ocean, we must learn to embrace its dual nature, finding strength and courage to face whatever comes our way.

8. Caught in the Downpour

Swamped every day, don't know what to say.

Even the colossal rain drops, won't let you to stay.

Do you even know what's keeping you drenched?

Stop holding the umbrella for others and don't get wrenched.

There are moments when the relentless challenges we face daily can leave us feeling utterly drained. Do you ever pause to consider what might be causing this distress?

Perhaps it's because we often prioritize the needs of others over our own well-being. It's essential to shift our focus towards self-care and refrain from allowing ourselves to be weighed down by the burdens of others.

It's akin to carrying an umbrella without realizing why we're still getting wet. Only later do we realize we were holding it for someone else, not ourselves. By prioritizing our own needs, we gain clarity and resilience to confront life's obstacles with greater confidence.

9. Rain's Release

Let us hear thunder, let us have some rain!
Let us see lightning, let us dance insane.
Wishing every raindrop, wash all your fears away!
Walking miles before things you could unsay.

After the rain and the fleeting showers,
The sun comes out as it hides behind its cover.
The clouds float away to find new bowers,
A gentle breeze and raindrops all over.

While I find comfort in watching the rain from indoors, I often dream of dancing in it. I wish each raindrop could wash away my many fears, including anger and secrets I keep hidden. When I watch the rain, I wish my worries were being washed away, leaving me feeling free.

When the rain subsides, stepping outside feels like embarking on a new journey. The air is infused with the earthy scent of damp soil, and the echoes of raindrops linger softly in the background. In this moment of tranquility, my troubles melt away, replaced by a profound sense of peace and clarity.

These moments remind me of nature's beauty and its ability to cleanse and renew. They give me hope that even in life's challenges, there's a chance for a fresh start. So, I find comfort in the rain, knowing it brings the promise of brighter days ahead.

10. Starry Slumber

The trees are at rest after a sunny day.
Listening to the twinkling stars, shining all their way
Awaiting a cool breeze to sing a lullaby.
Longing for a warm hug and a kiss goodnight's display.

As the day draws to a close, much like the trees settling under the gentle touch of twilight, there's a yearning within us to embrace tranquility. Just as the trees lean in to catch whispers from the stars, we too seek solace in the gentle embrace of our surroundings. Moments of serenity, similar to the trees awaiting the caress of a refreshing breeze, are what we all crave.

Life, much like the ever-changing weather, brings both moments of joy and times of adversity. Like the trees, our hearts long for love and compassion. These simple, yet profound, aspirations remind us of our shared humanity and the universal need for affection.

The trees, in their silent repose, serve as gentle reminders for us to seek inner peace amidst the chaos of life. Let us learn from their quiet wisdom, cherishing the conclusion of each day as an opportunity to unwind, reflect, and find solace in the beauty of existence.

11. Songs of Sunset and Stars

It's a warm hug to see the sunset,
The dusk loves you more than the heat during the day.
The setting rays shine bright in the sky,
As it gets warmer in the last resort.

All the little birds getting back from shore.
Some are sorry, some are alone.
Waiting for the dawn
To toil another day.

The night sky loves you more.
The cool winds heal the wound.
The stars shine brighter speaking a hundred words.
The new moon gives you a new hope to bloom.

I penned this poem to illustrate life's ever-changing nature, akin to the transition from day to night. As the sunset paints the sky, a sense of calm descends, signaling closure. Yet, we must embrace endings, for they pave the path for fresh beginnings.

Observing birds returning home at dusk serves as a gentle reminder—a new day awaits with boundless possibilities. Their flight whispers, "Today concludes, but tomorrow brings renewal."

Even amidst hardship, the prospect of a new dawn buoys our spirits. Tomorrow promises a chance for improvement, igniting hope and fortitude within.

In the nighttime hush, gazing at the starry expanse feels similar to soul medicine. The serene symphony of the night lulls us, fostering inner peace. And as the new moon graces the heavens, it serves as a beacon, reminding us of the perpetual cycle of new beginnings, even amidst darkness.

12. Blossom's Ballet

All the flowers bloom, it's the start of the day.
Waiting for the sunlight to clear its way.
The honeybees are dancing happy and gay.
Smelling the blossom, sucking the nectar away.

When the day starts, flowers wake up and open up. They wait for the sunlight to come and make everything bright. Happy bees fly around, going from flower to flower. They love the sweet smell of the blossoms and drink the nectar.

Bees help flowers grow by collecting nectar. This teamwork between bees and flowers is like a beautiful dance of nature, showing how everything works together to make the world a better place.

13. Twilight's Dance

The moon that shines so bright at night
Whom are you trying to impress?
The tiny plants shy away from the light.
Going to sleep in an instant.

Oh, little stars that hide during the day!
Too afraid of the Sun that glows all its way.
Waiting for the dusk to grab some attention.
There are millions of you seeking affection.

The bright moon in the night sky seems to want everyone's attention. But who is it trying to impress? Similarly, sometimes we feel like we need approval from others to feel good about ourselves.

On the flip side, fragile plants quickly hide from the sunlight, preferring to rest in darkness. This is similar to how we might feel stressed or scared by what's around us, choosing to find comfort in being alone.

The stars also hide during the day because they're afraid of the strong sun. Just like them, we might feel small or scared sometimes. But when the sun goes down, they come out again, looking for attention and love. It's like how we overcome our fears and show our true selves, wanting to connect with others and feel accepted.

Overall, the moon, stars, and plants show us how our inner thoughts and feelings can be like the things we see in nature. They help us understand the ups and downs of life and how we all want to feel loved and accepted.

14. Skyward Dreams

Clouds at great heights, want to touch, want to fly.

Like cotton candy, they float in the sky.

Wake up your inner child and jump up high.

Dream of resting on the clouds, drifting high and nigh.

Clouds make me feel like a kid again, filled with wonder and awe. They float high in the sky, like fluffy cotton candy, tempting me to reach out and touch them. Whenever I see clouds, I can't help but dream of flying among them, feeling weightless and free.

Imagining myself resting on the clouds, drifting higher and higher, fills me with a sense of adventure and excitement. It's like tapping into my inner child, letting go of all worries, and embracing the pure joy of the moment.

Clouds remind me to dream big and never lose sight of the magic that surrounds us every day.

15. Paths Untaken

In the journey of reaching the destination
Some thorns, some roses
But few paths will always remain untraveled.

Life presents us with a myriad of challenges, that have highs and lows. Sometimes things go well and sometimes they don't. We face challenges like problems, failures, or losing something important. But these tough times also teach us to be strong and keep going.

We learn how to handle difficulties and become better people because of them. Even though it's hard, we find ways to get through tough times and enjoy the good moments. Every experience, whether good or bad, helps us grow and makes our life story unique and meaningful.

Our journey towards a destination is not always smooth sailing. We encounter both challenges and moments of joy. These contrasting experiences contribute to the richness and complexity of the journey.

However, amidst the paths taken and experiences gained, there will always be some paths left untraveled. This implies that some opportunities or possibilities remain undiscovered or unexplored, adding an element of mystery and potential to the journey of life. Life reflects on the inevitability of facing obstacles and enjoying moments of beauty while acknowledging the unknown possibilities that lie ahead.

16. Frosty Morning Reverie

On a chilly winter morning,
When you snuggle in your bed,
With a duvet like a hug,
And a pillow beneath your head.

Stepping out, cup in hand, as the vapor hits your nose.
Feeling the mist, as you watch the saplings grow.
Awaiting the sunrise, as you nudge the little dew.
Singing with the birds, wondering when it flew.

I've grown fond of this piece of my work; it's become one of my favorites. Reading it takes me back to those cold winter mornings when all I wanted to do was snuggle up in bed under my warm blanket. It brings back memories of enjoying my favorite snacks in bed, wrapped up snugly while binge-watching TV shows.

For me, winter is the best season. I love the shorter days, the early sunset, and the excuse to stay in bed a little longer. I hope as you read this, you're reminded of your favorite winter memories.

Maybe you recall the gentle warmth of the sun creeping through your window in the morning. Or perhaps you remember the quiet streets as you made your way to school or work, listening to the birds chirping and feeling the crisp air on your skin.

We've all experienced those moments of blowing out cold air on a winter morning and pretending to be like the smoke from a chimney. These memories are precious, ones we can cherish and revisit time and time again.

17. Catching Life's Throw

When life keeps throwing stuff at you
Just keep catching them counting one and two.
You never know how, and you never know why,
You may never regret some things that passed by.

In the journey of life, challenges often arrive unexpectedly, reminiscent of trying to catch falling objects one after another. These hurdles may appear without warning, leaving us perplexed about their purpose or outcome. Yet, they are integral parts of our path.

At times, the significance of these experiences may elude us until much later. Upon reflection, we may discover that even the most arduous trials hold valuable lessons, ones we wouldn't trade despite their initial difficulty.

So, when faced with life's obstacles, strive to confront them methodically, tackling each one as it comes. Have faith that there's a reason behind every twist and turn, even if it remains veiled for now. Embrace the journey with open arms, recognizing that every experience, no matter how challenging, contributes to the mosaic of your being.

18. Glimmers of Spring

When spring arrives, the hours are longer.
You never realize when it got warmer.
Listening to the happy bird chirp
And the animals wake up from hibernation.

All the kids happy and merry
Waking up from the cozy winter sleep.
It's time to step out and play,
As the day is not ending sooner.

Feeling the cool breeze on your face
Watching the dusk fall.
And yearning for another bright day.
Eagerly awaiting dawn's first ray.

As spring comes, days get longer and warmer, but you might not even notice the change happening. You start hearing happy birds singing, which means nature is waking up from its winter sleep.

Kids are excited too, waking up from their cozy beds, ready to play outside because the days feel longer now. There's a feeling of endless possibilities in the air like the day will never end, and there's so much to explore.

When the sun starts to go down, the sky turns a beautiful golden color. You feel a nice breeze on your face, waiting for the next bright day to come. It's like nature is giving us a fresh start, filling us with hope and excitement for what's to come.

19. Smile's Symphony

Smile when you can, Smile if you care.

It's the simplest attire, easy to bear.

Smile a little extra and make somebody gay.

Smile to ease the pain and remember to pray!

They say a smile is the most precious adornment, and it comes free of cost. Often, people may seem unfriendly simply because they appear serious. Unfortunately, they're often misjudged because of this.

A smile holds incredible power to uplift anyone's spirits. It can turn a sad person's day around, spread happiness to all, and leave you feeling fulfilled for brightening someone else's day. Moreover, it can provide solace to someone in pain.

Even the smallest smile has the potential to dissolve someone's anger. Therefore, it's crucial to always remember the impact of a smile and to share it generously.

20. Summer's Glow

Summer is here,
The golden rays I see.
The blue skies shine brighter than ever.
Sunflowers blooming with glee.

So much work to do,
Sweltering hours to spend.
Tropical fruits for the rescue.
Happy I pretend.

Waiting for the night,
Longer are the days ahead.
As birds take their flight.
Waiting to hit the bed.

Summer brings joy and excitement with its sunny days and clear skies. Nature bursts into life with vibrant colors and fragrant blooms, like sunflowers turning toward the sun, spreading happiness.

For many, summer means outdoor fun and relaxation. Picnics, barbecues, and lazy days by the pool or beach are favorite pastimes. Longer daylight hours offer opportunities for water games and swimming, adding to the summer enjoyment.

One of the joys of summer is the abundance of delicious fruits and refreshing drinks. Watermelons, strawberries, and peaches offer a sweet escape from the heat. Cold lemonades, smoothies, and iced teas help stay cool and hydrated.

21. Fly Free

It could be now; it could be never.
You can make It big, sooner or later.
If you feel free, then spread your wings.
Soar like an eagle, feel like a King.

I've gleaned a few valuable lessons through experience, one being the importance of immediate action. Embracing the present moment and seizing opportunities for growth and success is crucial. Though timing can sometimes be uncertain, opportunities are often within reach.

Soaring like an eagle evokes a powerful sense of freedom and possibility. We need to liberate ourselves from self-imposed limitations to unlock our potential. And once you start realizing your dreams and start moving towards your goals there is a sense of empowerment.

Hence, I implore everyone that greatness is attainable for all, provided we are willing to take risks, embrace freedom, and pursue our aspirations with determination.

22. Shadows to Sunlight

• 43 •

The shadows in the dark, disappear slowly.
Yet fears emerge, creepy and crawly.
Neither prepared to confront the bright,
Nor ready to roll the fear of the night.

The night transitions slowly,
As the sun's rays travel through the glazing
Caught by surprise, all the fear is gone.
Waiting for the flowers to bloom strong.

As the shadows vanish in the dark, fears begin to emerge, crawling into our minds and making us uneasy. We feel unprepared to face the brightness of the day or to confront the fears that lurk in the night.

But as the night slowly transitions into the day, the gentle rays of the sun filter through the window, illuminating the room and dispelling our fears. Suddenly, everything feels lighter, and we find ourselves filled with hope and anticipation for what the new day will bring.

In this beautiful cycle of darkness turning into light, we are reminded that even in our darkest moments, there is always the promise of a brighter tomorrow. Just as flowers bloom after a long night, we too can emerge from our fears stronger and more resilient than before.

23. Fear's Revelation

• 45 •

What scares you in the dark is not the demons or the monsters
What scares you in the dark, is not the darkness itself.
What scares you in the dark, is not because you are alone.
But what is coming to light, and not ready to face your fears.

We all grapple with fears, anxieties, and worries that sometimes seem to loom larger in the darkness of night. It's those moments when sleep eludes us, and our minds wander into the realms of uncertainty. Yet, the unsettling aspect isn't the absence of light or the sense of solitude; rather, it's the apprehension of what lies within the shadows.

These fears aren't tangible threats like monsters or demons; they're the uncertainties that haunt our thoughts, the truths and vulnerabilities we conceal. The true terror stems from the prospect of facing these fears head-on, of confronting the realities we've long avoided. It's the anticipation of having to confront our deepest fears when they're finally brought to light.

In the darkest hours, it's not the darkness itself that unnerves us, but the prospect of confronting our innermost fears and vulnerabilities. Yet, it's through this confrontation that we find the opportunity for growth and resilience, gradually overcoming our anxieties and emerging stronger on the other side.

24. Journey's Echo

Away from home and far off you go.
Looking for a life and an abode.
Family and friends, waving goodbye.
With a sorrow heart and a gentle smile.

The fullness of time waiting ahead
Like the sun that shines before it sets.
Learning and growing with changes so quick.
Reminiscing good times that passed in a flick.

Heartful of vehemence, can't let it go.
Nobody behind to share this oh no!
Waiting to reunite and wanting to fly.
A hug and a cry, a loved one beside.

At some point, we all face the inevitable: leaving behind our loved ones. Whether it's for a job in a new city, relocating to a different country, pursuing education far from home, starting a new chapter in marriage, or even due to conflicts within the family, we embark on these journeys in search of a brighter future, filled with hope and anticipation. Yet, as we venture forth, we carry with us not only our belongings but also cherished memories that tug at our hearts.

In moments of solitude, we yearn for someone to confide in, to share our joys and sorrows, and to lend us a comforting shoulder to lean on. And amidst the tumultuous whirlwind of change, we realize that life must continue, despite the ache of separation.

This reflection was inspired by the Hindi movie "Dunki," which stirred up deep feelings and questions about life's transitions. It reminds us that even amidst uncertainty, there's always a glimmer of hope guiding us towards brighter days.

25. Mind's Reflection

• 49 •

Are you too busy to delve into your mind?
Or just forgotten you reside there too?
Too many in the multitude, and no room for more.
Wake up and free the lane, choose whom to ignore!

Sometimes, we find ourselves caught up in worrying about others—our friends, family, and those who depend on us. It's natural to want to help and support them, but in doing so, we often forget to take care of ourselves.

We've come to realize that it's crucial to prioritize our own well-being and mental health. Just as much as others need our attention and assistance, we also require time and space to tend to our own needs.

It's like our minds become busy intersections during rush hour, filled with thoughts and concerns competing for attention. The noise and chaos can become overwhelming, leaving us feeling frustrated and drained. Eventually, there's no room left for anyone else, including ourselves.

That's when we realize the importance of hitting the pause button and creating some breathing room in our minds. We need to clear the mental clutter and carve out moments of solitude for introspection and self-reflection. It's in these quiet moments that we can regain perspective, recharge our batteries, and reconnect with ourselves on a deeper level.

26. Echoes of Solitude

So much noise in the world
It's not the people around
Wait till you realize, it's you alone.

So much to talk about
So much to talk to
Turn around, and nobody.

Running to finish the race.
Running to reach the place.
Nobody to cheer you all the way.

Stepped out of the cocoon.
Built on the open nest.
Eagerly waiting for someone with zest.

Experiencing loneliness is like being adrift in a sea of faces, surrounded by people yet feeling utterly disconnected. Despite scanning the room, there's no one with whom to forge a meaningful connection, no soul to confide in or share innermost thoughts and emotions.

It's as though you inhabit a world of your own, distinct from everyone else, yearning for the warmth of companionship and the solace of understanding.

Navigating life's journey solo can be daunting, even amidst a bustling crowd. Despite the external clamor, an internal void persists, a yearning for someone to walk alongside you, offering support and encouragement.

27. Evening's Repose

Getting back to the nest after a weary day.
Let me quench my thirst, before I begin to sway.
Hey! The shoulders aren't ready to make more hay.
All I desire to do is hop in bed and lay.

Arriving home after a lengthy day brings a sense of relief, yet at times, attaining tranquility and repose proves challenging. We step through the door, wearied and longing for the comfort of our bed.

However, the weight of unfinished tasks looms large. Another chore awaits, adding to our burden and leaving us feeling overwhelmed and drained. It's as if the work is never-ending, and we can't seem to catch a moment's respite.

Yearning for a moment of respite, we find ourselves thwarted by the constant demands vying for our attention. It's a frustrating and exhausting cycle, leaving us craving a brief interlude to unwind and rejuvenate.

28. Tears to Pearls

Do you weep in the dark, hiding from everybody?
Every teardrop shine, Like pearls in the sea.
Wait for a little while, for miracles you will see.
Your troubles will get washed away,
Like a swash on the beach.

When the bitter changes to honey,
And you look back just to see.
You fathom the time and tears,
That went in vain just making you fear.

Do you ever feel like crying when you're alone in the dark? It's like every tear is precious, shining brightly just like pearls in the sea. But if you wait a little while, you'll see that things can get better. Your worries and troubles will fade away, just like the waves washing up on the shore.

Sometimes, when things seem bad, they can turn out okay in the end. When you look back at those tough times, you might realize that they weren't as scary as they seemed.

All those tears you shed might have felt like they were wasted, but they helped you become stronger. So, even when things seem hard, just remember that there's always hope for things to get better.

29. Mind's Melodies

In my mind, I talk a lot,
Dreams creep in, lost in thoughts:
Some gain wings, some do not
Waiting to soar, to high unknowns.

We all have endless thoughts in our minds like constant dreams. Sometimes it feels like thoughts have a life of their own, the continuous chattering and drifting.

Some of these thoughts that we have are like dreams that stay for a very short time and are ethereal. Some dreams linger and they refuse to leave our minds.

The ones that refuse to leave us are the ones that gain wings showing us they have a potential for an achievement. And these are the ones just waiting for an opportunity to reach the heights they aspire to.

30. Shattered Wings, Rising Phoenix

You want to gleam with your smile,

Release your pain and shine.

Waking with pride, cause nothing that happened was your fault.

Need more grace and dignity,

To walk around and parade.

Remind everybody out there you are back in line again.

Does it matter you are alone?

Gather the courage and pick up your broken wings.

Put the pieces together and shake off the dust.

Never look back, there are miles before you stop.

Sometimes, all you want is to smile, to let go of the hurt, and let your happiness shine through. You wake up with a sense of pride, knowing that whatever happened wasn't your fault. You hold your head high, determined to show the world that you're back and stronger than ever.

Even if it feels like you're all alone, you have to find the strength within yourself. Gather up the broken pieces of your spirit and piece them back together. Brush off the remnants of past pain and struggles. Don't dwell on the past; instead, focus on the journey ahead. There's still a long road to travel, but with every step, you're moving closer to a brighter future.

Remember, it's okay to feel lost or discouraged at times, but never lose sight of the resilience and determination that lie within you. Keep pushing forward, knowing that every obstacle you overcome brings you one step closer to your goals. You have the power to rise above any challenge and emerge stronger on the other side. So, hold onto hope and keep moving forward, one step at a time.